Family learning
The foundation of
effective education

Titus Alexander

First published in
November 1997

by

Demos
9 Bridewell Place
London EC4V 6AP
Tel: 0171 353 4479
Fax: 0171 353 4481

Arguments 15

ISBN 1 898309 98 1

Contents

Acknowledgements

These ideas and arguments are based on 45 years experience as a family member, twenty years as a community education worker, and eight years as an education adviser and inspector with particular responsibility for family learning. I owe a considerable debt to parents, teachers and thinkers from whom I have learned much, particularly Frances Sansom and Mary Crowley of East London Parent Link; Gillian Pugh, Hetty Einzig and other members of the Parenting Education Forum; Alwyn Morgan, Diana Stoker, John Bastiani, Pat Moss, Roger Hancock, Ruth Merttens, Sheila Wolfendale, Tanny Stobart and other members of the National Home School Development Group; Alan Tuckett, Sheila Carlton and others associated with the National Institute of Adult Continuing Education. I also owe much to the research represented by the books cited as references. I would like to thank Dr James Tooley for inviting me to make the case for families as a place of learning in the first place, Professor David Hargreaves for his comments on an early draft and Tom Bentley of Demos for seeing its way to publication. And to my parents. I am of course entirely responsible for all mistakes.

Titus Alexander
August 1997

Imagine an education system where none of the educators are trained. Indeed, where training is seen as a sign of weakness. There is no curriculum but the amount to be learned is vast and it is assumed that everyone knows what it is. There is no assessment, but if people fail the penalties are severe. This is not any old education system but the foundation for every course, job and profession in the world. It is, of course, the family.

Parents are the most important educator in any person's life, yet they get most of the blame when things go wrong and little support or training to ensure that all children get the best possible start in life.[1]

Titus Alexander, 1995

Executive summary

Families are the foundation of education. Children spend less than 15 per cent of their waking time in school between birth and school leaving age. Parents and other carers are responsible for 85 per cent of a child's waking time. Many studies show that home background is the biggest influence on children's learning. Differences in support for learning at home are probably the greatest source of inequality in educational attainment among children of equal ability.

Family learning refers to the vast amount of learning which takes place in and around families, from personal development, language acquisition and hobbies to the process of becoming a teenager, parent, step-parent or grandparent, or taking other family responsibilities.

Most public spending for education goes on schools and colleges; parents get very little support for their responsibilities as a child's first educator. Less than 5 per cent of parents participate in parenting education programmes at any time in their lives. Provision is largely funded and organised by parents themselves, supported by a patchwork of short-term, insecure sources. Few schools have a systematic approach to involving all parents in their children's education.

Most public spending on families goes on child protection, coping with families under stress or the consequences of family failure. There is very little help to prevent problems from becoming a crisis.

Increased support for parents as children's first and most enduring educators would bring significant improvements in educational achievement as well as helping to reduce mental illness, crime, drug abuse and violence. Active support for family learning could create a virtuous cycle of positive personal development, higher achievement, increased earnings, greater well-being and ultimately more cohesive communities.

The following recommendations are directed at everyone who works with parents and children. National and local government have a strategic role in providing leadership and a framework for local action but schools, local education authorities (LEAs), health authorities, social services, the criminal justice system, employers, trade unions, television companies, voluntary organisations and parents themselves can all take initiatives to promote family learning.

This paper presents a long-term strategy for supporting family learning, based on the many local and national initiatives across the country. Lead agencies, action points and funding are briefly mentioned in italics. More details are provided in chapters six, seven and eight.

Recommendations for action

1. A national media **Campaign for Family Learning**, along the lines of the BBC's adult literacy campaign *On the Move,* to raise the status of parenting, support parents' central role in education and encourage people to participate in parenting programmes and other family learning activities. *The government, television and parenting organisations could take the lead to create a small central campaign team, identify local organisers and pump-prime provision through the National Lottery, Millennium Commission or other funding. Spending under £10 million a year could have a huge impact.*

2. **Affordable parenting education and support programmes** for all who want them, with a built-in long-term independent evaluation programme. Parent Network, Family Caring Trust, Exploring Parenthood, National Society for the Prevention of Cruelty to Children, HomeStart, Newpin and many other groups offer parenting programmes. *Parenting education forums and providers could take the lead, with funding from the National Lottery, local and national government, charitable trusts, long-term sponsorship and parents themselves. Annual costs would depend on uptake, rising from current low levels to about £200 million a year. Long-term evaluation would be conducted by research institutions and funded by the ESRC.*

3. **Local learning plans** to develop facilities for family learning all year round, such as play areas, after school clubs, public libraries, galleries, museums, adventure playgrounds, urban farms, youth clubs, sports grounds, multimedia and 'electronic village halls', with

funding from the National Lottery. *Local government would take the lead in partnership with local statutory and voluntary agencies.*

4. **Strengthen family support networks** through health visiting, support groups, pre-schools, nurseries and voluntary organisations to develop confidence and mutual support, including targeted provision for families in difficulty and those with fathers in prison. *Local government would coordinate this through Children's Services Plans, Early Years Plans, Drug Action Teams, Learning Cities and parent education forums.*

5. **Easy access to help and support** through helplines, parent support groups and child guidance. *Local government or parent education and support forums would coordinate provision.*

6. Improve recognition, accreditation and training for **community teachers,** such as pre-school leaders, parent education facilitators and mentors. *Education authorities and accrediting bodies will take the lead.*

7. **Strengthen school partnerships with parents** by developing whole-school policies for supporting parents, including termly meetings of all parents in a class, a parents' representative forum, regular information on the curriculum and on how to support children's learning and local family education workers. This needs national support from a small team, guidelines, training and GEST/Standards funding. *Schools would take the lead, supported by LEAs, local authorities and the Department for Education and Employment. National support would cost about £150,000 for a central unit, £10 million to £20 million for GEST/Standards funding, £40 million to £60 million for partnership responsibility posts and £40 million for non-contact time. A family education worker at every school would cost about £1 billion.*

8. **Enable schools to become community centres for lifelong learning,** open all day, all-year round, offering summer schools, holiday and after school activities, family support, adult education and recreation and access to libraries, computers and the Internet. *Schools would be supported by LEAs and national government, with a mixture of funding from the Further Education Funding Council, National Lottery, local taxes and users.*

9. Improved coordination of family policy and provision at local and national levels through:

- integrated neighbourhood family centres
- local inter-agency family service planning, including Early Years Development Plans
- a national family policy forum and interdepartmental planning within governments.

10. **Family-centred economic and employment policies** to increase family incomes, enable family members to spend time together and include domestic labour in economic indicators.

Public investment in support for parents would lead to significant improvement in educational attainment as well as savings in child protection and other areas of public spending. Parents and children who experience the benefits of education are also likely to increase earnings and invest more of their own income on education. *The total cost of these proposals is less than the increase in spending on higher and further education under the previous government.*

The Appendix outlines a **National Family Learning Initiative** to lead this strategy by building on local initiatives through:

1. a high-profile public information campaign, promoted through television
2. a national telephone support-line to refer people to local provision
3. a package of training and support for local agencies to share expertise and best practice
4. a national network of trained family learning coordinators
5. seed funding for local family learning initiatives.

The recent allocations of lottery funding for family literacy, out-of-school activities and Family Learning Millennium Awards provide a starting point for a coordinated national initiative.

1. Introduction: why family learning matters

Education is the government's number one priority. The Labour manifesto also commits it to strengthening families. David Blunkett speaks passionately about family learning. All this is encouraging, but the government has not yet shown that it understands the central importance of families as *places of learning*.

Once families are recognised as the foundation of learning, a far-reaching transformation of institutions which work with children and parents will begin. Parents will be treated as the lead agents in the care and education of children, with training and support like every other agency working with children. Schools will see their role as extending and enhancing family learning, strengthening and supporting the foundation of learning at home. All agencies concerned with families will see their priority as supporting parents as children's first and most enduring educators.

Family learning refers to the vast amount of learning which takes place in and around families, from the first smile, word and step to the complex transitions of adolescence, becoming a parent, looking after elderly relatives or coping with bereavement. A more detailed definition is laid out in *Riches beyond price: making the most of family learning:*

'Family learning is as varied as families themselves. For the purposes of this paper it is worth identifying five distinct aspects of family learning:

- informal learning within the family
- family members learning together
- learning about roles, relationships and responsibilities in relation to the stages of family life, including parenting education
- learning how to understand, take responsibility and make decisions in relation to wider society, in which the family is a foundation for citizenship
- learning how to deal with agencies that serve families, such as schools, social services, voluntary organisations and the criminal justice system.

> The common feature of these five aspects is that they
> involve intergenerational learning based on kinship,
> however defined. This definition is not determined by
> function but by the complex continuity of relationships that
> is the essence of human life.'[2]

Active encouragement and support at home has a significant impact on educational attainment at school. Unless parental support increases, the government's ambitions to improve education will also fall short. To avoid failure, the priority for education policy must be to support families as the foundation for learning.

Family learning also connects many other strands of government policy that are usually tackled separately, if at all. Personal happiness and mental health are closely linked to family experiences. Family breakdown imposes considerable personal and public costs. There is evidence for links between criminal behaviour and parenting. Economic prosperity and employment increasingly depend on knowledge, skills and flexibility, which in turn depend on educational achievement that is rooted in family learning. All of these issues are closely connected with poverty, social cohesion, social justice and social exclusion.[3]

Education and inequality

Education is essential to improving the life chances for the most disadvantaged. Inequality between home backgrounds is still the greatest source of inequality in educational attainment. The question is, what will do most to raise achievement among those who currently achieve least? This question is not new. Over a century ago, similar concerns about global competition and social exclusion led to the extension of primary education and to university reform. Secondary education was extended in 1944 for similar reasons. Thirty years ago, the Robbins Report advocated the expansion of higher education to strengthen the economy while the Plowden Report proposed Education Priority Areas to tackle deprivation.[4] In the past decade, an avalanche of reforms has tried to raise education standards. Yet our educational and economic performance still lags behind many European and Asian countries. The reason why a century of reforms have not met the dual challenges of social deprivation and global competition is that the importance of families for learning has not been fully addressed. Support for families as places of learning provides a powerful way of tackling a number of central problems facing British society.

2. Families as places of learning

Between birth and school leaving age children spend less than 15 per cent of their waking time in school. Of this, about a quarter is spent in the playground. Each child in a group of about 30 gets relatively little individual attention from a teacher. Those who demand more are often seen as difficult or disruptive.

Parents and carers are responsible for the other 85 per cent of a child's waking time. They can, if they choose, give children undivided attention far longer than any teacher. This has vital consequences for children's development. For example, children who participate in family mealtime discussions develop the highest aptitude for reading and vocabulary. One large-scale study showed that mealtime conversations use ten times more sophisticated words than other situations, including school lessons and playtimes.[5]

About half of a person's intelligence and learning ability develops by the age of four, and 80 per cent by the age of eight.[6] The home is more important than schools for translating this intelligence and learning ability into educational achievement.[7] For almost all measures of scholastic attainment, differences between schools account for far less than features of the family or home.[8] There is a 'very strong relationship between knowledge of literacy at age five and all later assessments of school achievement.'[9]

Social class often appears to be a significant factor in differences in school attainment, with children from professional and white collar backgrounds making significantly greater progress at school than other groups.[10] While 80 per cent of young people from professional backgrounds go to university, the proportion from unskilled lower-income families is only 10 per cent. But studies of successful young professionals from poor families show that enthusiastic parental involvement in their education is the common characteristic, regardless of social class.[11] A longitudinal study of almost 7,000 people born in 1958 suggested that there was less correlation between private education and occupational attainment than often assumed. 'What matters, it seems, is good parenting, irrespective of the class or education level of the parents, and good parenting can be found in all social classes.'[12] This same study indicated that individual ability and motivation are key factors in success.

The importance of parenting is supported by US research which showed that 'non-authoritarian attitudes and child-centred parenting coupled with a strong positive attitude to the child's education far outweighed the effects of any other factors.'[13] Similar evidence convinced American educator Earl Shaefer to switch his attention from classrooms to living rooms, declaring that 'parents should be recognised as the most influential educators of their own children.'[14]

A consistent aspect of successful schools is parental support for children's learning.[15] One of the most rigorous accounts of school effectiveness states that all studies which have compared the relative importance of home and schools 'have clearly shown that for almost all measures of scholastic attainment, the differences between schools accounted for far less of the variance than did features of the family or home.'[16] This is almost certainly a major factor in the difference in educational attainment between countries. On the continent, it is usual for all parents to meet with the class teacher as a group once or twice a term to discuss the curriculum and other issues. In many countries, each class elects one or two representatives to a parents' council. Several countries have strong national parents' organisations and national or regional consultative bodies with statutory rights to discuss and recommend amendments to legislation on education. The higher levels of achievement in Japan, Taiwan and South Korea reflect parents' commitment to education at least as much as teaching methods.

Moreover, success in school does not necessarily mean that people understand what they appear to know or can apply what they have learned. Children learn how to 'conform, and even play the system, but many do not allow the knowledge presented to them to make any deep impact on their view of reality.'[17] Even successful university students can have fundamental misconceptions about basic ideas within their subjects and base their thinking on concepts developed before they started school.[18] At every level, research evidence points to the home as the foundation for learning throughout life.

3. Schools and family learning

'Life skills' courses have become increasingly prominent in many school, college and training programmes. Concern about crime, drug use and teenage pregnancy is raising the profile of personal, social and health education (PSHE), as well as preparation for parenthood in schools.[19] All these programmes deal with attitudes and skills which it was once assumed were acquired at home. But these courses are a tiny proportion of the school timetable, they usually have low status within the curriculum and are often taught by teachers with little or no training in these subjects. As the school curriculum becomes overcrowded, more attention must be given to the home as a place of learning. However much policy makers and educators want to pack into the school timetable, it can never be more than a small proportion of a young person's learning experience. We cannot replace families themselves as the place where life skills are learned. If parents are in difficulty, they need to be supported, not supplanted.

In many British schools there is relatively little constructive communication between teachers and parents. Most communications between home and school are instructions *from* school *to* parents, mainly about administrative matters. Parents are often treated as instruments for the delivery, discipline and domestication of school children, not as the *primary* partner in education. Sometimes parents are told what they can do to help the school. More rarely are they actively involved in their child's learning or asked for their views. Communication about educational matters focuses almost entirely on the school's view of the child. Apart from annual parents' evenings, many parents are only invited to meet the teacher when things have gone wrong.

Teachers cannot be blamed for the low quality of relationships between home and school. Work with parents usually has to be done in a teacher's own time on top of a full timetable. Most teacher training courses do not cover parental involvement. School funding takes no account of the time needed to build home–school links. Government policies and guidelines have not emphasised partnerships with parents. The treatment of parents in the Ofsted Framework for Inspection is very limited and inspection reports are inconsistent and inadequate.[20]

The previous government's requirement for schools to draw up a Home–School Contract appeared to be designed to exclude 'difficult' parents rather than to support all parents. The Code of Conduct for children with special needs provides an excellent model for work with parents, but it only applies to a few children. A growing number of schools recognise the importance of working with parents, but often as a desirable extra rather than as a central task. Few schools see the partnership with parents as an essential responsibility which requires as much effort, preparation and skill as teaching itself.

The unprecedented changes in curriculum, structure, funding, inspection and testing over the past decade have been enormously expensive in terms of morale as well as money. Even more is needed to improve premises, technology, training and staffing. But none of these reforms took account of the fundamental importance of home as a place of learning. This is like redecorating a house while the foundations crumble.

Compulsory free schooling has been one of the biggest collective investments in Britain this century. Yet most young people, endowed with an innate capacity to learn, have achieved far less than their full potential when they leave school. In 1993, almost 15 per cent of 21 year olds had limited literacy skills, 20 per cent had very limited competence with elementary maths and many more needed help with basic education. Although the proportion of young people leaving school with qualifications has risen above 93 per cent, less than one third of British sixteen year olds reach the equivalent of GCSE grades A to C compared with half of sixteen year olds in Japan and two thirds in France.

A good school *can* give children a huge advantage in life. National as well as international comparisons show that good schools make a significant difference in the education and life chances of both individuals and countries. The book, *School matters*, demonstrated that 'disadvantaged children in the most effective schools can end up with higher achievements than their advantaged peers in the less effective schools.'[21] Studies of effective schools clearly show how learning can be improved through positive leadership, shared goals, an attractive and stimulating environment, high expectations, good teaching, parental involvement and other features.[22] Children who lag behind can be given extra help which is neither punitive nor demeaning.

But schools alone cannot be expected to cure the ills of society or even to raise achievement on their own. They must be part of a learning partnership with parents and all other agencies that work with families and children. This means in practice that we must begin by looking at the family as a place of learning in more detail.

4. Effective families

Although families vary widely, there are three basic requirements for an effective family, of which the first is by far the most important:

1. effective relationships
2. time
3. permitting circumstances, in terms of a home, income and community support.

It is much harder to bring up children in adverse conditions, such as in poor housing, on a low income or as a lone parent, but we know that effective relationships based on secure attachment between child and parent can overcome the most difficult circumstances. Effective relationships are undoubtedly the most important aspect of parenting and often the most difficult.

The basic need of every child to grow up in a loving home may seem obvious but addressing this issue directly is almost taboo.

Many parents feel pressured and guilty about their ability to give children what they need. Professionals who work with families under stress quite rightly do not want to stigmatise or blame parents. The result is that discussions about what children need from parents get pushed aside or polarised into a moralistic, defensive slanging match. Instead of moralising, we need an open, honest debate about what works within families and to offer parents and carers unconditional support so that all children get a secure start in life.

Much has been written about the damaging experiences of childhood and the therapies which seek to heal them. Much less effort has gone into finding out what enables a family to ensure that children grow up healthy and happy. Reginald Clark's research into well-motivated high achievers from low income black families in the United States concluded that 'effective families' made the largest contribution to success in later life:

'Like effective schools, effective families have a set of easy-to-identify characteristics. These cut across family income, education and ethnic background. They remain true for single parent and two parent households and for families with working and non-working mothers. Effective families display a number of positive attitudes and behaviours towards their children which help them to succeed in school and in life.'[23]

Robin Skynner, former Chair of the Institute of Family Therapy and co-author of *Families and how to survive them*,[24] identified seven characteristics of 'basically healthy families'. These are:

- a positive approach to life, often evident through humour, fun and enjoyment
- a strong commitment and sense of involvement, closeness and intimacy
- a capacity for individual members to be independent and happy on their own
- open, frank and clear communication between family members
- firm control of family activity by parents, following consultation to accommodate all points of view as far as possible
- equal power between parents who resolve issues easily and amicably

- an ability to cope with change and loss, including the death of loved ones.

This could be described as the basis for a 'core curriculum' of family life. Different cultures have family norms which do not fit this model at every point, but they are effective because they are accepted and provide genuine security to family members. Many parenting education programmes have independently developed a 'family curriculum' consistent with Skynner's seven points. *Confident parents, confident children*,[25] a comprehensive survey of policy and practice in parent education in Britain, summarises their main features in a very similar list:

- a belief that 'good enough' parents are responsible, authoritative, assertive, positive, democratic and consistent
- they are neither autocratic, authoritarian nor permissive
- parents' strengths should be reaffirmed, building on confidence and self-esteem
- parents need to know *what* needs to be done (knowledge) and *how* to do it (skills), but they also need to feel confident they *can do it* (attitudes, particularly self-esteem)
- experience and feelings are as important as knowledge
- the importance of the relationship between two parents is emphasised, as is the impact of this relationship on the children
- the impact of how parents were themselves parented is acknowledged
- there is an emphasis on increasing understanding and enjoyment of children, and on parents' role as their child's first educators
- development of skills for handling children's behaviour, such as encouraging good behaviour, rather than focusing on bad behaviour, creating boundaries, being consistent, handling conflict, offering choices, improving communication skills and listening reflectively
- an approach which suggests strategies, rather than giving answers.

These approaches to parenting education do not see the parent educator as a superior source of knowledge. Most educators are parents themselves whose aim is to support parents and help them improve communication within families so that differences can be resolved more easily.

An effective family is not perfect – there is of course no such thing as a perfect family – but it is 'good enough' to provide a secure start in life. The critical issue is how society can ensure that all families are able to provide the emotional security every child needs.

5. The costs of failing families

In crude terms, the average child contributes about £800,000 to the economy over his or her lifetime, at today's prices. Children who do well contribute many times this amount. On the other hand, a child who is abandoned, abused or turns to crime can cost society millions of pounds. The ability of parents to provide a safe and positive environment for children to grow up is not a purely private matter. We all benefit or suffer from how well a child is raised.

Not all family learning is positive. About 750,000 children in Britain suffer long-term trauma as a result of domestic violence.[26] Three out of ten women are likely to be injured by their partners at least once during their lifetime. Some 60,000 women and children flee to women's refuges and safe houses each year. On average, over 80 children are murdered every year, most of them by other family members. Over 35,000 children are on the Child Protection Register, two fifths of whom are under five. About 7,000 cases of sexual abuse are reported annually. Every year, 43,000 people under the age of 17 run away from home and are reported to the police. On present trends, a quarter of children born today may see their parents divorce before they are sixteen years old. One in eight adults were beaten or abused as children. Many more suffered from constant criticism or emotional neglect. One in seven people suffer severe mental health problems at some point in their lives, one in three experience mental illness of some kind and every year almost a million people seek help from counsellors, therapists or the Samaritans, often tracing their distress to experiences within the family. Numerous studies record the pain of growing up in unhappy families.[27]

Misery in family life is not the result of malice. Parents do the best they can. Most love their children but often they themselves did not have a secure, loving childhood. They simply pass on the lessons learned at home. As the poet Philip Larkin put it:

> They fuck you up, your mum and dad.
> They may not mean to, but they do.
> They fill you with the faults they had
> And add some extra, just for you.

Much of this suffering could be reduced if parents could communicate better with each other and their children. But instead of investing in support for parents as a child's most important educator and carer, most public spending on families is on coping with the consequences of failure.

Family crisis services
Each year, over £2 billion is spent on services to children and families (excluding treatment for physical illness). Of this just 15 per cent is spent on community health services (mainly health visitors) while three quarters is spent by social services on child protection, residential care and fostering. A relatively small amount is spent on family centres, nurseries and preventative work. In other words, most money spent on children and parents is crisis intervention. This is expensive: the average cost of a child in residential care is over £660 a week, foster care costs over £150 a week and each child protection case costs thousands of pounds. Children in families under stress are also likely to achieve least at school and to have most difficulty in later life, in terms of employment, mental and physical health and criminal behaviour. Relationships within families are not the only cause of stress. Employment opportunities, housing conditions, poverty and physical illness matter enormously.

Many family services are over-stretched and under-funded, struggling to meet growing demands. But they are like emergency services at the foot of a dangerous cliff. Relatively little is done to stop people from falling over the cliff in the first place.

Prevention is a complex process, but one of its most important challenges is to enable people to bring up children within a secure, loving home, as outlined in the previous chapter. This is more easily said than done. At present, most professional public services implicitly teach people that teachers, nurses, doctors and other professionals are better at doing things than they are. Training in the caring professions treats people as a case, a recipient and object of professional expertise. Parents who question services or want to be more involved are often criticised, openly or subtly, as pushy, demanding or difficult. These attitudes are changing, but for families in crisis, professional services often seem remote and confirm their sense of powerlessness and failure. Most parents have relatively little choice about the public services they use or how they are run. Intervention by social services is a sign that something is seriously wrong, particularly when linked with statutory investigations into abuse or neglect. Many services are not seen as a source of support but as a confirmation of failure for parents who probably experienced failure in school, relationships, work and other areas of their lives. For some young men in particular, one way of achieving success is criminal activity. Affairs with women and fathering children can be another. For some young women, having a child gives them self-worth and value.

Blaming parents does not help. Family failure has often been created over generations through many factors, including male violence, poverty, lack of opportunities and the erosion of self-esteem, personal relationships and mutual support upon which healthy families depend. Parents who want support or advice often do not know where to turn. Asking for help sounds like admitting that you cannot cope. Many are afraid of interfering officials and the risk that their child may be taken away. Finding help or advice is often a haphazard voyage of chance and frustration through a bewildering patchwork of agencies. For a parent standing at the top of the cliff, feeling depressed, isolated or even violent towards their child, jumping over sometimes seems the only way of getting help.

Unfortunately there is rarely a safety net, just a tangled snare. As the Audit Commission reported in 1994, community health and social services are often badly coordinated and poorly focused, and do not involve parents sufficiently.[28] Child and adolescent mental health services are also characterised by poor dialogue, lack of collaboration and an absence of strategies.[29] Cooperation between education and social services is often minimal or difficult, as each profession speaks a different language and pursues a different purpose.

Better coordination alone will not deal with the results of our failure to recognise the importance of families. Community health, education and social services must take a more strategic and *educational* role in enabling families to deal with problems. This means designing services round families' needs for learning and support, rather than expecting families to fit in with priorities of the caring professions. It means turning public services into partnerships, in which parents are treated as the primary agent in children's lives and can learn to fulfil their responsibilities. Education has a central role in enabling people to develop skills in communication, parenting and relationships. What this might mean in practice is described in the next chapter. Coordination of services is dealt with in chapter eight.

6. Building the foundations of a learning society

What can be done to enable all families to become effective places of learning? The next three chapters present a long-term strategy for strengthening the foundations of a learning society by fostering children's natural capacity to learn within a family. This requires a national campaign to promote family learning, affordable parent education available to all parents, and local support networks with a family centre in every area. It also means transforming schools to involve parents in a much closer partnership (outlined in chapter seven). To underpin this strategy, we need better inter-agency planning and cooperation to provide stability and innovation in response to changing needs, as summarised in chapter eight.

A campaign for family learning

Radio and television have the greatest potential to change attitudes towards parenting education and to support families as places of learning. Carlton Television's annual 'Better Parenting Awareness' weeks use 60-second snippets to convey supportive messages to parents, prompting over 7,000 Londoners to ring for further information in just one week. The BBC and the Basic Skills Agency received over 300,000 requests for help following a short national television campaign for family literacy. The Open University offers excellent courses in parenting, but at higher costs to learners. In practice, *Coronation Street*, *EastEnders*, *Brookside* and *Neighbours* are the most pervasive family education on television. They could take a lead in making parenting education acceptable and accessible by including a parenting programme in the story line and by promoting a telephone helpline after episodes which deal with family learning.

The potential of television to act as a catalyst in education was powerfully demonstrated by the BBC's highly successful adult literacy campaign *On the Move* in the 1070s. Short populist programmes raised awareness about the issue and gave thousands of people the confidence to seek help for reading and writing difficulties. The programmes and the national support centre – now the Basic Skills Agency – helped to transform adult literacy and basic skills from a marginal, often voluntary, movement funded by charities into a significant part of mainstream provision. Now, almost every adult and further education service offers adult literacy classes, free of charge, funded as a national priority.

A national parenting education television campaign could likewise transform parenting and education. It would raise the status of parenting, increase awareness of parents' central role in education and encourage more people to join parenting programmes and support groups. For a national campaign to be effective, it needs a small central campaign team, local organisers and affordable courses in all areas. This would mean a substantial increase in both training and provision. Funding would be essential for the central team, but, as with *On the Move*, the very decision to launch a national television campaign would generate support and funds at a local level from a wide range of sources, including parents themselves. It could cost less than £10 million to launch a major campaign for family learning with far-reaching impact. Appendix 1 outlines the key features of a national initiative to champion family learning.

Affordable parenting education and support programmes

Less than 4 per cent of parents participate in any form of parenting education during their lives.[30] Most parenting education programmes are run by voluntary organisations like Parent Network and groups using Family Caring Trust materials.[31] They are led by parents or volunteers rather than professionals, although many volunteers are also teachers, health visitors or community workers. Many parenting programmes for the general public tend to be more available to middle class parents who can afford to pay and are also less likely to fear intervention by social services. Many local authorities are beginning to fund parenting programmes. As a result, they are now being run successfully by African Caribbean, Asian and working class parents in Birmingham, Plymouth, Waltham Forest and other areas. A growing number of agencies are also funding targeted programmes like the Family Nurturing Network in Oxford, Mellow Parenting in London and Scotland, or the Radford Shared Care Project in Nottingham to work with parents experiencing stress or severe difficulties in parenting. An important area of targeted provision is in prison, particular for young fathers, like the 'Dads R Us' course at Lancaster Farms Young Offenders Institute, run in partnership with the YMCA.

Most evaluations of parenting programmes[32] show almost universally positive reports from the parent participants. The main benefits are increased self-confidence or self-esteem, better understanding of their own and children's behaviour and improved parenting skills. Several studies of target provision, such as the Parent–Child Game used by Maudsley Hospital, also show improvements in children's behaviour for a year or more after the course.[33] There have been no rigorous long-term studies of parenting programmes in Britain, which would be essential if provision were to be increased.

There are no national standards or qualifications for parenting education programmes. Many are led by parents whose main qualification is that they can use the materials published by the Family Caring Trust. The Parent Network, Newpin, Parents as Teachers and most other providers have their own training and accreditation programmes. The Parenting Education and Support Forum is investigating all aspects of training and accreditation in order to establish benchmark standards. Accreditation is a sensitive area, because one of the strengths of many general programmes is that they are run by members of the community based on a philosophy of mutual support and peer education. On the other hand, parenting programmes can trigger recall of profound and sometimes traumatic experiences in parents' own childhood, which a facilitator must be capable of handling sensitively and safely.

The importance of parenting is so fundamental for personal development that parenting education and opportunities for family learning should be available to all who want it. Estimates of how much should be invested in parenting education and support range from 0.5 per cent to 3 per cent of the education budget. The National Children's Bureau estimated that one particular approach, based on the Hampshire Job for Life model,[34] would cost about £170 million a year, about 0.5 per cent of the education budget. This would provide one worker and a team of volunteers to serve the catchment of each secondary school.[35] Tim Brighouse, Chief Education Officer for Birmingham, has suggested that 1.5 per cent of the education budget should be devoted to supporting parents for the 85 per cent of time they are responsible for children.[36] A more ambitious programme (and thus more realistic in terms of educational outcomes) would have the equivalent of one family learning support worker per primary school. This would cost almost £1 billion, about 3 per cent of the education budget. Even if this was partly funded by parents, it would still require substantial public support.

Extending facilities for family learning

Families also need a wide choice of affordable activities, courses and provision to develop creativity, curiosity and communication skills. Public libraries, galleries, museums, parks, botanical gardens, play centres, after-school clubs, adventure playgrounds, urban farms, performance areas, community theatre groups, sports grounds and nature areas are essential for children to develop skills and interests outside home. The decline in public libraries, play spaces and sports grounds is at least as damaging to learning as increased class sizes or poor teaching. Similarly, organisations like the Scouts and Guides, Woodcraft Folk and youth services provide valuable opportunities for informal learning but in many areas they have lost funding or been squeezed out of school premises. On the other hand, many private and public facilities are becoming more welcoming to families, from shops and pubs with children's areas to activity centres like Alphabet Zoo. In many areas, local authorities or the local press compile guides to activities for children and families, particularly in school holidays.

Many of these facilities come under the heading of leisure and recreation. They are often seen as less important than education, employ less qualified staff and are more likely to suffer cuts in funding. But in practice these services can stimulate enthusiasm for learning among parents and children as much as school can. Opportunities for informal learning all year round should be developed and sustained with the same commitment formal education is given if we are to value diversity and the all-round development of human potential. Trained staff or volunteers in small neighbourhood play areas, local branch libraries and parks can make a big difference in encouraging children to use their energy creatively and involving adults in activities with children. The scope for family learning facilities has scarcely been explored. We need *local learning action plans* that embrace all facilities for informal learning, setting standards for access, provision, staff training and variety of opportunities, as well as promoting participation by the public.

Television, computers and the Internet are making new resources for learning increasingly accessible, but their potential is largely untapped and many families cannot afford access. Initiatives like cybercafés and 'electronic village halls' in Manchester are increasing access to computers and the Internet. As more schools go on-line, the service could be made available to the local community outside school hours. An Internet terminal in every family home would be a desirable and feasible education policy objective early in the next century. But much more important than the technology are skilled teachers who can inspire and guide young people to make the best use of these resources.

Developing community teachers

A vital and often under-estimated element in education is the stimulus and support of individual teachers. Inspiring teachers and mentors enable people to transform their lives, while poor teachers can damage them for life. Developing personal potential involves many different teachers throughout life. Child minders, nursery nurses, play group leaders, story tellers, doctors, foster parents, community leaders, religious figures, sports coaches, librarians, managers, therapists, police, probation officers and all other professions are engaged in some kind of teaching from time to time. Trained Parent Link coordinators, pre-school organisers and class rooms assistants are 'lay teachers' who can make a profound impact on people's lives.

At some stage every job or role in society involves sharing the experience of one generation with the next. Good teaching is one of the most powerful ways of encouraging a desire to learn. Improving skills, status and support for all kinds of teachers is essential in a global economy where information and understanding are the keys to success. Enabling more people to develop teaching and mentoring skills as part of their work will also help them to reflect, consolidate their experience and develop their own knowledge to meet changing circumstances. A learning society would enable many more people to develop the skills of coaching, facilitating, mentoring and teaching in every occupation.

Community teachers should be recognised through the national system of accreditation and training as having a distinctive role. Their skills are different from conventional teaching, with more emphasis on one-to-one coaching, small group work, learning through doing and projects – skills which could also benefit schools. To be fully effective, community teachers need to be part of a comprehensive system of family support networks.

Strengthening family support networks

The strongest support networks are created by people committed to each other, whether out of a sense of affinity, community, duty or love. Neither private nor public services can make this kind of commitment unconditionally. Commercial relationships last only as long as there is money to pay for them and people with the greatest needs are least able to buy support. Public services are able to support people regardless of ability to pay, but even the best services have financial and institutional limitations which make it impossible to give long-term commitment to an individual. Ultimately, only family and close friends can do that and even they may find it difficult. Economic and social change is driving an increase in many people's mobility. This makes it even more important to secure resilient support networks to make family life more viable, enjoyable and educational.

The more that support is based on competence and commitment the more resilient it will be. Such support flourishes best when people know each other and have a shared involvement, where they can meet to talk things through and where they have the necessary time and resources. The five most important steps to create effective family support networks are:

- actively reaching out to people with children, particularly first-time parents
- funding community-based support groups
- providing easy access to help and support in times of difficulty
- ensuring that every family has easy access to a family centre of some kind
- targeted support for parents under stress or in difficulty.

The following paragraphs describe each of these in turn.

Actively reaching out to people with children is vital. Looking after a baby, particularly the first, can be very lonely and difficult for many mothers. The birth of a child can put strains on a relationship or trigger conflicts within the extended family, and many mothers have very little personal support. Fathers, in particular, need to learn how to care for children and their mothers from before birth. Health visitors and voluntary schemes such as community mothers, parent mentors and Homestart can offer valuable support. In Birmingham, health visitors give every family with young children an introductory pack with a book, poster and information on local services as part of the Bookstart project which involves health trusts, libraries, the university, education department, TEC and others.[37] Similarly, home visits by a teacher or educational visitor in the year before school starts can encourage learning and build a partnership between home and school.

Second, families need easy access to help and support when they first experience difficulties. Advice lines offer confidential information and counselling at the end of a phone, but take-up is low. One survey found that just 1 per cent of parents said they were most likely to seek advice from a helpline. They are most likely to turn to friends and neighbours (56 per cent), their mother (47 per cent) or a doctor or health visitor (38 per cent) for help. The same survey reported that parents felt they most wanted self-help groups (44 per cent), parent education groups (33 per cent), family centres (32 per cent) and professional counselling (31 per cent).[38] Very often parents simply need reassurance or someone to listen while they talk through worries.

When parents experience more serious difficulties in their relationships with their partner or children, they may find it difficult to seek help. Doctors, teachers, childminders and childcare workers are often in a position to offer support or refer people to an appropriate agency. This is a skilled role, for which the charity One Plus One has developed training called Brief Encounters for health professionals to offer appropriate support when people turn to them for help.[39] In educational terms, this 'relationship coaching' is a vital learning process which often happens informally but can also be taught.

Equally important are sources of more sustained support such as counselling, parent support groups, marriage guidance, bereavement counselling and self-help groups. When parents experience difficulties with family life they often trigger unresolved issues from their own childhood, so someone who seeks help for apparently slight problems should never be ignored. Early support can arrest generations of distress.

Voluntary support groups run childbirth classes, parenting education, pre-schools and community nurseries which develop confidence and competence within families. Homestart, Parent Network, Pre-School Learning Alliance and many other groups offer parents support from trained volunteers or paid staff, and opportunities to become trained helpers themselves. Many mothers find their way back into education and employment through voluntary work and training offered by these agencies, creating a virtuous cycle of personal, social and economic regeneration around childcare. The close relationship between experience, learning and application as well as peer tutoring means that these support groups make a very significant contribution to a learning society.

Fourth, neighbourhood family centres can create a focus for family services within a neighbourhood. Centres like Pen Green in Corby offer a supportive environment for both children and parents, including a nursery, play-schools, support groups, drop-in sessions, legal advice, counselling, adult education classes, health clinics and a wide variety of activities in response to changing community needs. As with most provision for families and children, many of the participants are women, but changes in employment mean that growing numbers of men are reassessing their roles and taking greater responsibility for childcare. At their best, family centres bring together the whole range of family support services and agencies within a single site, enabling different agencies to learn from each other as well as from users. Many family centres grow out of voluntary initiatives funded through a range of sources, including education, health, social services, the former Urban Programme, trusts and fees. Where family centres are targeted at particular groups, such as families at risk, they can get a negative reputation as a stigmatised service. This makes it important for family centres to be developed and publicised as a universal service, like schools and healthcare.

The government's commitment to set up 25 Early Excellence Centres is encouraging but these must be part of a long-term strategy to establish a family centre of some kind within buggy distance of every parent. In many areas, it may be possible for health clinics, nurseries, community centres or primary schools to become multi-purpose family centres. But the biggest challenge is transforming professional attitudes to create real partnerships with parents.

Fifth, **targeted provision** for families in crisis, parents at risk of abusing or neglecting their children, or fathers in prison are an essential part of family support networks. Where parenting education and support is a normal thing for parents to do, as part of the process of having children, targeted provision is likely to be more acceptable, attracting more self-referers before difficulties get out of hand.

7. Transforming schools

The transformation of our schools is probably the single most important task in securing the long-term prosperity and well-being of this country. As I have argued, school improvement is not enough. Unless all parents are actively involved in their children's education, a growing proportion of teachers' time will be remedial.

Changing relationships between school and home could be the most constructive starting point for schools to transform themselves. A national family learning campaign to promote the importance of parents, as discussed earlier, would also influence schools. But schools could support families as the foundation for learning by treating parents as partners in children's education and becoming community education centres, serving all ages, owned and governed by the communities they serve.

If education services become more focused on the process and outcomes of learning and less preoccupied with structures and status, then schools of the future will be even more varied than today. The following sketch focuses on how the relationship between families and schools might develop. Many of these approaches can be found on a small scale already. The challenge is to make them a widespread reality.

Supporting parents as a child's first educators

Most parents know their child better than any teacher. At school age, parents are responsible for children for four to five times more waking hours than they spend in school. In my experience of interviewing hundreds of parents, most want more advice on how to help their children learn. Many parents furtively help their children by buying books at W H Smiths or Boots, anxious not to be seen to be undermining the teacher. Even on poor, working class estates some parents employ private tutors to give their children extra help at home. Many black and ethnic minority groups run supplementary schools to provide additional education for their children. At the same time, some parents believe that teaching is the school's job and children should be free to enjoy childhood outside school hours. In many cases these parents, or their parents before them, had been scolded by teachers for doing maths, reading or writing the 'wrong way' in the days when primary schools had a line in the playground to exclude parents.

Today most schools involve parents to some extent, particularly in the early years. But in order to involve parents as equal partners in their children's education, every school needs to include parents in all aspects of the school, from its overall development plan to daily lessons. Varying circumstances mean that each school would need to draw up its own policy to meet the needs of its staff, parents and children. There are also a number of benchmarks which every school could be expected to work towards. These are:

1. a welcome and induction programme for new parents, starting well before their child begins school
2. a baseline assessment of each child involving parents and teacher together, to develop individual learning plans for each child, clearly identifying what the school and parents will do
3. clear information on what children are being taught and how parents can help

4. regular home learning activities
5. advice and training on how to help children learn at home
6. termly meetings for each parent and child to discuss progress with their teachers
7. recognition of the diversity of languages, cultures and abilities in any school community
8. class meetings of all parents with the class or form teacher
9. a parents' council with two representatives from each class or year
10. a parent partnership post with some non-contact time to develop work with parents.

Home–school contracts, required under recent legislation, could prove counter-productive unless they are developed with parents as part of a comprehensive partnership. It would be worthwhile for parents and teachers to spend time talking through their respective expectations when children start school. A home–school agreement or understanding could then be a valuable record of the conversation. There is a useful role for contracts with children and parents as a way of dealing with specific issues. The new government's decision to review the introduction of contracts is a sign of maturity. What we need are guidelines for a whole school approach to working with parents along the following lines.

The **welcome and induction** parents get when they first bring their child to nursery or school can determine their relationship with education for the rest of their lives, and the next generation as well. It is therefore worth investing time and effort to establish trust, to emphasise parents' importance as educators and to offer guidance for learning at home. A growing number of nurseries and schools include a home visit as part of the induction programme. In an ideal world, class teachers would act as a learning consultant to a group of eight or ten families from birth or three years old, offering parents support and encouragement long before their child starts school.

Before children start school, parent(s) and child would meet with their teacher to make a **joint assessment** of what the child can do and could be encouraged to learn next. This 'baseline assessment' would be used to draw up a personal learning plan, which would be kept by the parents and used as a reference point for future meetings with the teacher. This joint assessment would be repeated every term. Parents experiencing depression or difficulty with their child's behaviour could be introduced to a support group or parenting programme.

Clear information on what and how children are being taught, with specific guidance on how parents can help, is particularly important. One constructive approach in primary school is for children to review what they have learned at the end of each day, so that they can answer the inevitable question, 'What did you do in school today?' and continue the discussion at home.

Home learning activities are an essential bridge and channel of communication between home and school, and can start in nursery. Home learning activities need to be much more varied and stimulating than traditional homework. Again, parents need much more specific guidance on how to make the most of homework, with a home learning journal to communicate with parents and help children learn how to plan, work independently and use evaluation effectively. The communications revolution means that a growing number of parents and teachers will communicate through the Internet, increasing the possibility of supported independent learning throughout the year.

Class meetings, rather than Parent Teacher Associations, should be the keystone of work with parents, as at Rushcommon School in Abingdon or many continental schools. This involves teachers and parents of each child meeting as a class once a term or half-term to discuss the curriculum, progress and anything affecting the class as a whole. The Danish Dialogue exercise, translated by Glasgow University,[40] is an excellent means of building partnership through these meetings. Class meetings would also include advice on how parents can help children at home and, in the older years, provide opportunities to discuss difficult issues such as drugs, bullying, sex, further education and employment.

Each class meeting could elect two representatives – male and female – to a **parents council** for the whole school. This would be much more representative than most PTAs and would focus primarily on educational and broad policy issues.

Termly **parent–teacher consultations** need to be taken more seriously as a means of focusing on the specific gifts and needs of each child, involving children themselves from about the age of nine.

To support the development of a whole-school approach to working with parents, each school needs a **parent partnership coordinator**, together with training and support from the local education authority.

These nine points are only a broad outline for home–school partnerships. A huge variety of imaginative activities with parents takes place in many schools already. Peers school, for example, runs an Early Education Partnership called PEEP, working with parents and children from birth to nursery age to build self-confidence and learning skills.[41] Dale Primary School Family Learning Programme runs evening events on science and technology for the whole family which are regularly oversubscribed.[42]

Projects like these need to be disseminated and developed. In many schools, work with parents tends to involve only a handful of parents in each class. A realistic home–school policy would aim to engage *every* parent in a minimum core of activities, just as good teachers aim to include every child in their lessons.

Support for home–school partnerships

Developing a whole school policy for work with parents is more complex than implementing a new reading or maths scheme, a new initiative like Technical and Vocational Education (TVEI) or National Vocational Qualifications (NVQs). It touches on every aspect of a school's work and needs at least equivalent support from education advisers, officers and teachers as the core subjects or special needs.

Local authorities like Devon, Hertfordshire, Newham, Liverpool and Oxfordshire have parent support programmes and experienced advisers from whom the rest of the country can learn. Most authorities have partnership projects for special needs, providing more models for work with all parents. The government's renewed commitment to local education authorities must make parent partnerships a core task of LEAs.

At a national level, work with parents needs active support by a small team, guidelines and training materials[43] with GEST/Standards funding for local authorities to provide training and support. Partnerships with parents should also be a central focus of teacher training, school inspections and the national curriculum as it is revised. This would cost about £40 million to £60 million for partnership responsibility posts, £40 million for non-contact time, £10 million to £20 million a year for GEST/Standards training and £150,000 for a central unit to promote parent partnerships.

Several national voluntary organisations also support work with parents, like Education Extra or the North Yorkshire District of the Workers' Education Association, which has developed a highly successful accredited course for voluntary helpers in school that is now available in many parts of the country.

The next step would be to train and appoint family education workers for every school or cluster of schools, starting in Education Priority Areas where achievement is lowest. This would eventually cost almost £1 billion a year. But it would make a striking contribution to the standards and quality of education among children and adults, as well as significantly cutting the costs of failing families.

Home schooling

Any discussion of family learning raises questions about home schooling. According to Education Otherwise, the charity which supports parents educating children at home, at least 25,000 families in Britain do so. This is less than 0.5 per cent of all school-age children. The role call of illustrious names who were educated at home is impressive, including Louisa May Allcott, the Brontë sisters, Agatha Christie, Noel Coward, Gerald Durrell, Doris Lessing, CS Lewis, the six Mitford sisters, Yehudi Menuhin, George Bernard Shaw, Beatrix Potter, Sue Townsend and Mary Wesley. But it is highly unlikely that more than a tiny minority of parents could either afford or wish to educate their children at home. What is possible, however, is that families might prefer greater variety of smaller, more flexible places of learning as radically different relationships develop between home, school and other agencies.

The logical step from parental choice of schools is the right of parents and learners to choose where, how and what they want to learn. This might include making portage available to parents who for one reason or other want to educate their children away from school (portage schemes provide materials for children to learn at home or in hospital due to illness or other special needs). Schools should also be allowed to admit pupils (and adults) on a part-time basis, so that children learning at home can attend school for certain subjects, such as languages, science or sport. The essence of education is not schooling so much as the ability of a skilled teacher to draw out the learner's gifts and inspire them to fulfil their potential as human beings. This is a role which good schools can perform for whole communities.

Schools as community centres for life-long learning

Critics of schooling rightly draw attention to the negative experience many people have of it. But when we consider practical and cost-effective ways of ensuring that each generation is introduced to the vast range of skills and knowledge needed in the world today, there is much to be said for an organisation dedicated to learning and teaching. Schools can support disciplined study, particularly in subjects which are not intuitively obvious or which benefit from systematic instruction. Schools also give young people opportunities to build relationships beyond their family or immediate community, to learn how to work with other people and to develop shared values essential for society to maintain cohesion. However, to retain public confidence, schools must become more effective, flexible and family-oriented. We need a new vision of how schools might develop, not just as well run institutions of instruction, but as a democratic learning community in a comprehensive system.

The major feature of a family-centred learning society is that *every* school, public library and many other facilities would be community education centres, open all day for most of the year, providing resources and support for learning to all family members, as and when they want to learn. At present, many school premises are used for learning during less than three quarters of their potential opening hours. This is a colossal waste of facilities and public investment. School libraries, workshops, computer rooms and other facilities could be used much more widely, as in some community schools. This would break down barriers between home and school, turning school premises into a focus for community celebrations and neighbourhood democracy as well as places of learning. Schools would be respected as places where people develop skills and deepen their understanding of the world through participation as well as study. Children and parents would bring questions and problems to learn about in school and all could work together at the frontiers of knowledge as well as on basic skills. Grandparents and other adults would be actively involved. But to build this wider vision we need to start with what exists and first ensure that all parents are active participants in education.

Funding for family learning and schooling

The greatest inequality in education spending is not between private and state schools, but between home backgrounds. Educational inequalities between families are not primarily financial, although finance plays a part, but involve social and cultural priorities about how people spend their time and money. This is not a question of social class, so much as culture and family traditions. There are working class families who, with very little income, always valued learning, discussion and activities as a family, just as there are rich families where parents have no time for their children and can afford every distraction available, from multimedia to fast cars.

These differences in emotional and economic resources at home outweigh other inequalities in education spending. They are amplified through the school system, where parents' abilities to move house, raise funds, lobby or otherwise choose and improve schools within the state sector are at least as important as the ability to pay private school fees. The present funding system for state schools effectively perpetuates inequalities in family background because it assumes everyone starts equal and then allocates roughly equal resources for each pupil. Until inequality in family learning is addressed, school improvement will always struggle to cope with social circumstances beyond its influence.

As a society, we need to spend much more on education. In a knowledge, skills and communication-based global economy anything less than continuous investment will disadvantage future generations. And if learning at home has the most influence on educational outcomes, then the priority must be to spend more on family centres, parenting education and learning at home, particularly in areas where educational achievement is low. But we also need to improve school premises, reduce class sizes, buy more books, keep pace with technology and enable staff to improve their skills and knowledge. In many areas, significant numbers of children need one-to-one tuition and very small classes if they are to make progress. However, increasing state spending by the amounts needed may be impossible within the present system.

We therefore need to think more creatively about ways of attracting more resources into education, particularly for family learning. State spending could never equalise the resources to the level available in the most affluent homes, but the *way* in which state spending is allocated could make a huge difference to parental commitment to education and ensure that every child gets the support they need to achieve their potential. Greater flexibility in how people pay for schooling could enable more public funds to be directed towards educational needs and priorities.

Although more state spending is desirable, it is not necessarily the best or sole solution to increasing resources for education. Education is not just a service, but a process in which people participate. Ultimately, what people learn is what they make their own. Giving people a direct stake in local provision for education could encourage a more active interest in the nature, costs and quality of what is provided.

Many people already choose to pay for satellite or cable TV, computers and courses in fitness, football, arts, complementary medicine, sports, parenting education or personal growth. Public libraries charge for videos, computer games and CDs while lending books free of charge. Adult education and leisure services juggle with multilevel price scales. Many schools hire out their premises or even run evening classes at commercial rates. State schools raise hundreds of millions of pounds a year from parents, a few raising over £100,000 in covenants. Some voluntary aided schools charge surreptitious fees under the name of donations that are all but compulsory. The mixed economy is already a reality in state education. Most people spend more on education at home and in school than appears in the public accounts. The question is, how should this be done in the best interests of universal education and social justice?

One possibility is that in future the state might fund educational premises and essential running costs, leaving people to pay by subscription or local education rates, assessed on a sliding scale by income. Inequality between geographical areas would be addressed through the school funding formula and the local government Standard Spending Assessment. By focusing on educational needs and outcomes, this system could bring more funds into education overall *and* reduce inequality.

Control over finance is a crucial test for community ownership, local democracy and public participation. Radical thinking is also needed if all parents are to have real power over local provision and address inequalities within each area. To increase community ownership and commitment to schools, families need real ownership and control. Local management of schools has dramatically shifted power and responsibility from the town hall to heads and governors. There are still teething problems but devolved powers will not be removed. Many schools want more responsibility for maintenance and capital spending. In the United States, school boards campaign for public agreement to borrow money or raise local taxes through local referendums, so that major education spending decisions are taken by the whole community.

The ability of parents to choose and participate in their child's schooling is an extension of their natural involvement in learning at home. Making a financial contribution of some kind would deepen the sense of ownership. Parents on social security and low incomes would be exempt, but they should benefit from the overall increase in resources within the state education system.

But schools are only part of a mosaic of organisations concerned with learning and families. Health, leisure, libraries, social services and other agencies have an important role in supporting family learning. We therefore need a vision of how these agencies can work together.

8. Coordinating family policy and provision

Chapter five raised far-reaching questions about the role of the agencies which work with children and parents in crisis. It pointed to the role of parenting education and support in helping to prevent difficulties becoming crises and the importance of agencies working in partnership with each other and with parents. This chapter briefly outlines the kind of local and national structures needed to support family learning.

Almost every inquiry into child abuse has revealed inadequacies in inter-agency coordination. Conflicting agendas at a national level have also made it difficult to develop support locally, as education, health, housing, social services and criminal justice pull in different directions and economic policies undermine the lot.[44] Four measures to develop coherent support for family learning are:

1. the creation of integrated neighbourhood family centres
2. integrated planning of family support services at a local level
3. effective government structures for children at national level
4. family-centred economic and employment policies.

Neighbourhood family centres
The most tangible way of supporting families as places of learning would be to create family centres in every neighbourhood as a base for local family services and a source of advice, education, support and community activities, as described in chapter six. In *Championing children*, the National Children's Bureau describes one possible model, illustrated in Figure 1.

Coordination of family services
Neighbourhood family centres make inter-agency cooperation visible and accessible but it is also important that it is backed up by joint planning at all levels. Coordination of support for families is

Figure 1. Support for families with young children: a locally based model

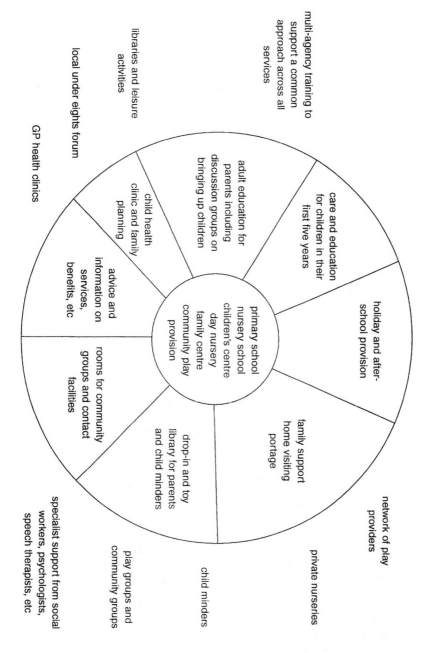

multi-agency training to
support a common
approach across all
services

libraries and leisure
activities

local under eights forum

GP health clinics

adult education for
parents including
discussion groups on
bringing up children

child health
clinic and family
planning

advice and
information on
services,
benefits, etc

care and education
for children in their
first five years

primary school
nursery school
children's centre
day nursery
family centre
community play
provision

rooms for community
groups and contact
facilities

drop-in and toy
library for parents
and child minders

holiday and after-
school provision

family support
home visiting
portage

network of play
providers

private nurseries

child minders

play groups and
community groups

specialist support from social
workers, psychologists,
speech therapists, etc

Source: Rea Price J and Pugh G, 1995, *Championing children*, Manchester City Council, Manchester.

improving as a result of the 1989 Children Act, but it needs to involve children and all agencies that affect their lives, including housing, transport and leisure services,[45] as well as parents as the primary 'agencies' involved in childcare.

The government's proposal to fund provision on the basis of integrated Early Years Development Plans is an excellent start.[46] But joint planning is often difficult. It takes time to build trust and mutual understanding and can easily be broken through the lack of tangible results or disputes over funding and responsibilities. Valuable lessons can be learned from the Single Regeneration Budget process, Children's Service Planning, Learning Cities and action on drugs as set out in *Tackling drugs together*.[47] This otherwise excellent model of inter-agency cooperation failed to involve parents sufficiently and therefore reduced the effectiveness of drugs education[48]. Participation by parents and local level liaison must be built into planning and provision to ensure that services are responsive. The basis of cooperation also needs to be spelled out in a protocol for partnership, as used by some Learning Cities, to reduce the rivalry which mars many joint initiatives.

The US state of Washington offers a rare example of an attempt to coordinate family services. The legislature set up a state-wide Family Policy Council on which all agencies that work with families are represented, from education and health to the juvenile justice system, together with elected representatives. This structure is reproduced at local level. Every county of about 40,000 people has a Community Network of 23 people, ten from the different agencies and thirteen representing different community interests. The council and each network has a responsibility to plan for the area. They have powers to vary departmental funding criteria so that funds can be allocated flexibly to meet specific needs of the area. The Family Policy Council and Networks were set up in response to rising juvenile crime, drug use and children at risk but their scope includes recreation, creativity and all family services. These 'policy focused networks' aim to cut across departmental boundaries and develop joint strategies for all agencies which work with families, to give users more direct access to strategic decision making. Breaking down functional barriers between institutions is fundamental to

Further reading

Alexander T and Clyne P, 1995, *Riches beyond price: making the most of family learning,* National Institute of Adult Continuing Education, Leicester.

Alexander T, Bastiani J and Beresford E, 1996, *A practical guide to home–school policies,* JET Publications, Ruddington.

Clark R, 1983, *Family life and school achievement: why poor black children succeed or fail,* Chicago University Press, Chicago.

Pugh G, De'Ath E and Smith C, 1994, *Confident parents, confident children,* National Children's Bureau, London.

Smith C, 1996, *Developing parenting programmes.* National Children's Bureau, London.

Utting D and others, 1993, *Crime and the family,* Family Policy Studies Centre, London.

Wells G, 1986, *The meaning makers.* Hodder and Stoughton, London.

Key contacts

Education Extra, 18 Victoria Park Square, London E2 9PF, tel: 0181 983 1061/980 6263

Exploring Parenthood, 4 Ivory Place, Threadgold St, London W11 4BP, tel: 0171 221 4471

National Home-School Development Association, 67 Musters Road, Ruddington, Nottingham, NG11 6JB, tel: 01159 845960

Family Caring Trust, 44 Rathfriland Road, Newry, Co. Down, BT34 1LD

Family Policy Studies Centre, 231 Baker St, London, NW1 6XE, tel: 0171 486 8211

Parenting Education and Support Forum, c/o National Children's Bureau, 8 Wakley St, London, EC1V 7QE, tel: 0171 843 6099

Parent Network, Room 2, Winchester House, Kennington Park, 11 Cranmer Road, SW9 6EJ tel: 0171 735 459

Appendix 1. Proposals for a national initiative on family learning

Support for family learning is an entirely new sector of education which is growing throughout the country. In some areas it is relatively well developed, with a network of agencies and staff working together to support families at a local level. In other areas there is very little education and support available to parents. Most of the country has some provision but it is fragmented and uncoordinated.

A national family learning initiative would act as a catalyst to strengthen local cooperation and increase support for families with relatively few additional resources. The strategy could be developed by a small national team with experience of working with schools, local communities, health visiting, crime prevention and family support. It would be overseen by a steering group drawn from leading agencies involved with family learning and television, supported by panel of senior politicians and staff from all departments which work with families in order to tackle administrative or legislative obstacles.

The initiative would support and build on the diversity of local initiatives through:

1. a high-profile **public information campaign**, promoted through television
2. a national **telephone support line** to refer people to local provision
3. a package of **training and support** for local agencies to share expertise and best practice
4. a national **network of trained family learning coordinators** working locally
5. **seed funding** for local family learning initiatives.

Elements of this framework already exist piecemeal in many parts of the country. The National Family Learning Initiative would aim to develop each of these strands in partnership with relevant local and national agencies. Recent grants by the National Lottery and

Millennium Commission have begun to fund a bottom-up drive to develop family learning projects. A national initiative would give them coherence and strength.

Appendix 2. A few words about 'the family'

In this paper, the word 'family' means a long-term intergenerational relationship. It includes foster families, single parents and same-sex partners with children as well as married couples with children. Ideally, families are based on the love, mutual support and life-long commitment of adults with both parental and filial responsibilities within a network of friends and relations. Most families are complex relationships across generations and geography, linked by lineage, loyalty, love or accidents of procreation. Few families are quite alike, even among the majority of two parents with dependent children. Some families experience long continuity through history and wide connections across society. Others exist fleetingly through fraught encounters during court-ordered contact time or long-distance phone calls between footloose parent and free-range offspring. Whatever the circumstances, our earliest experiences imprint themselves deeply on our behaviour and capacity for learning throughout life.

The realities of family life vary so greatly that it is about as useful to talk about 'the family' as it is to talk about 'the meal'. Nutrition, taste and enjoyment depend on ingredients, skill and, above all, the company round the table. So too with families, in all their diversity. Culture, income, education and experience make a difference to family life, as they do for food, but the quality of preparation and conversation are decisive to the outcome. Just as there are general principles for cooking, so there are general principles for living which can be learned. The central issue is not 'the family' but the conditions which enable people to flourish as families. Sustaining a family is much more difficult than preparing a meal, yet there are many more books, classes and television programmes about cooking than about living as a family. Family life, like good food, entails hard work as well as skill, but its purpose is to contribute to creating pleasure and well-being. Learning to stimulate joy through family life is a worthwhile goal.

Demands and expectations of family life have changed enormously throughout history. The way we live has been transformed over the past 30 years by modern contraception, feminism, new technologies, advertising, television, the social security system, changing employment patterns and a significant rise in disposable income for most men and women. Families are still more stable than during most of history apart from the Victorian era. Before then a majority of children were bereaved of at least one parent by the time they were adult. A quarter of all marriages were a remarriage for one partner and over a quarter of families included step-children.[49]

Two distinctive features of family life in late twentieth century Britain are also worth noting. First, families today are primarily concerned with leisure and consumption rather than production and mutual welfare. Few families are held together by economic necessity. Children have no economic responsibilities and may have little experience of a meaningful role or purpose in their own right. Second, few families are significant social institutions in their own right. Indeed, a peculiar feature of Western families is the way in which each family is seen as beginning with the birth of a child, expressed by the phrase 'starting a family'. Historically, marriage usually meant one person (normally the bride) leaving her family to join another, or two families joining through matrimony. Families which start as a result of two individuals having children are very different from extended families into which children are born – which is the reality, however much it may be denied.

Many traditional views of families seek to control family members in order to make them fit society as they see it. In my view, families have the potential to be a crucible of responsible freedom, enabling individuals to fulfil their potential and shape society as free and equal citizens.

About the author

Titus Alexander is an independent educator and author who works in all phases of education. As a research assistant at Sussex University he developed a course on Learning to Learn. He was a community worker in Brighton and London, a Principle Lecturer in the ILEA and then Adviser for Community Education for the London Borough of Waltham Forest. He is an accredited Ofsted inspector and co-author of Riches beyond price: making the most of family learning, and Home-school policies: a practical guide. He edited *The self-esteem directory: a guide to policy and practice* (1997). Other publications include *Know university* (1976), *Value for people: adult education and popular planning* (1986), and *Unravelling global apartheid: an overview of world politics* (Polity Press, 1996).

He is a founder member of the Self-Esteem Network and Parenting Education & Support Forum. He is also a maker and teller of stories for children.

Notes

[1] Alexander T, 1996, 'Learning begins at home' in Bastiani J and Wolferdale S, eds, *Home-school work in Britain*, David Fulton, London, 15.

[2] Alexander T and Clyne P, 1995, *Riches beyond price: making the most of family learning*, NIACE Policy Discussion Paper, National Institute of Adult Continuing Education, Leicester.

[3] For more on this see Bentley T, 1997, 'Learning to belong' in Demos Collection 11, *Tackling social exclusion*.

[4] Robbins Committee, 1963, *Higher education*, HMSO, London Central Advisory. Council for Education (England), 1967, *Children and their primary schools* (The Plowden Report), HMSO, London.

[5] Catherine Snow, Harvard University Graduate School of Education, reported in *Times Education Supplement*, 2 February 1996.

[6] Bloom BS, 1964, *Stability and change in human characteristics*, John Wiley, NY.

[7] See note 3.

[8] Rutter M and Madge N, 1976, *Cycles of disadvantage*, Heineman, London.

[9] Wells G, 1986, *The meaning makers*, Hodder and Stoughton, London, 147.

[10] Mortimore P et al, 1995, *School matters: the junior years* ,Paul Chapman Publishing, London, 132, 133.

[11] Bloom BS, 1985, *Developing talent in young people*, Ballantine, New York.

[12] Saunders P, 1994, National Child Development Study, cited in ESRC, 1995, *Annual Report 1994/95*, ESRC, Colchester. See also Saunders P, 1994, *Social mobility in Britain: an empirical evaluation of two competing explanations*, University of Sussex, Brighton.

[13] Osborn AF, 1990 'Resilient children: a longitudinal study of high achieving socially disadvantaged children' in *Early Childhood Development and Care*, vol 62, 23-47.

[14] Shaefer E, 1970, 'Need for early and Continuing Education' in *Education of the Infant and Young Child*, New York; Shaefer E, 1972, 'Parents as educators: evidence from the research' in *Young Children*, New York.

[15] Rutter M and Madge N, 1976, *Cycles of disadvantage*, Heineman, London, cited in Rutter M at al, 1979, *Fifteen thousand hours*, Open Books, London, 6; see also Henderson A, 1987, *The evidence continues to grow: parental involvement improves student achievement*, National Committee for Citizens in Education, Columbia, Maryland.

[16] See note 9, 289.

[17] Barnes D, 1975, *From communication to curriculum*, Penguin, London, 17.

17 Gardner H, 1993, *The unschooled mind: how children think and how schools should teach*, Fontana Press, London, esp ch 8-12.

[19] NSPCC Cymru/Wales, 1996, *Education for parenthood: resource pack*, NSPCC Cymru/Wales, Cardiff (available from NSPCC Cymru/ Wales, 9 Brindley Rd, Cardiff, CF1 7TX); Sharland P and Hope P, 1997, *Tomorrow's parents*, Children's Society and Gulbenkian Foundation, London.

[20] Unpublished 1997 study by the National Home School Development Association, 67 Musters Road, Ruddington, Notts NG11 6JB.

[21] See note 9, 217.

[22] National Commission on Education, 1993, *Learning to succeed*, Heineman, London, 142; see also Sandy A, 1990, *Making schools more effective*, CEDAR Papers 2, University of Warwick, Warwick; Mortimore et al, 1995 (note 9); Rutter M at al, 1979 (note 14); National Commission on Education, 1995, *Success against the odds*, Routledge, London.

22 Clark R, 1983, Family life and school achievement: why poor black children succeed or fail, University of Chicago Press, Chicago.

[24] Skynner R and Cleese J, 1983, *Families and how to survive them*, Cedar, London.

[25] Pugh G et al, 1994, *Confident Parents, Confident Children*, National Children's Bureau, London.

[26] NCH Action for Children, 1994, *The hidden victims: children and domestic violence*, NCH Action for Children, London.

[27] Cooper D, 1967, *Psychiatry and anti-psychiatry*, Tavistock, London; Cooper D and Laing RD, 1964, *Reason and violence*, Tavistock, London; Laing RD, 1971, *The politics of the family and other essays*, Tavistock, LONDON; Miller A, 1987, *For your own good: the roots of violence in child-rearing*, (1st edn 1983) Virago, London.

[28] Audit Commission, 1994, *Seen but not heard: coordinating community child health and social services for children in Needs*, HMSO, London.

[29] Health Advisory Service, 1995, *Together we stand*, Health Advisory Service, London.

[30] Smith C, 1996, *Developing parenting programmes*, National Children's Bureau, London.

[31] *Parent Link* course run by Parent Network, Parent Network, Room 2, Winchester House, Kennington Park, 11 Cranmer Road, SW9 6EJ Tel: 0171 735 459.

[32] See note 29, ch 6.

[33] Webster-Straton C, 1984, 'Randomized trail of two parent-training programmes for families with conduct disordered children' in *Journal of Consulting and Clinical Psychology*, vol 42, no 4, 666. See also Webster-Straton C and Herbert M, 1994, *Troubled families, problem children*, John Wiley, Chichester.

[34] Pugh G and Pouton L, 1987, *Parenting as a job for life*, National Children's Bureau, London.

[35] See note 24, 93.

[36] Tim Brighouse, Times Education Supplement, 19 July 1996.

[37] Bookstart can be reached care of CORE Skills Development Partnership, 100 Broad St, Birmingham B15 1AE, tel: 0121 248 8083.

[38] Sainsbury's Family Survey, *Sainsbury's The Magazine*, May 1994.

[39] *One Plus One* can be reached at 12 New Burlington Street, London, W1X 1FF, tel: 0171 734 2020.

[40] *Dialogue,* Department of Education, 8 University Gardens, University of Glasgow, G12 8QQ, Primary and secondary versions £23.50 each. *Early years dialogue*, £15 from Learning Initiatives, 32 Carisbrooke Rd, London, E17 7EF

[41] Rosemary Roberts, Coordinator, PEEP, Peers School, Sandy Lane West, Littlemore, Oxford, OX4 5JY.

[42] Allan Randall, Dale Primary School, Porter Road, Derby, DE27 6NL, Tel: 01332 2760070.

[43] Titus Alexander, John Bastiani, Emma Beresford, *Home school policies: a practical guide,* available from JET publications, 67 Musters Rd, Ruddington NG11 6JB,£14.95

[44] For more on the need for cross agency co-ordination, see 6 Perri, 1997, *Holistic government*, Demos, London.

[45] Sutton P, 1995, *Crossing the boundaries*, National Children's Bureau, London, 68.

[46] Labour Party, 1997, *Early excellence: A head start for every child*, Labour Party, London.

[47] Lord President of the Council and Leader of the House of Commons, 1995, *Tackling drugs together: a strategy for England, 1995-98,* Cm 2846, HMSO, London.

[48] Roehampton report, *Drugs education: a parent's needs study,* cited in, 'Parents ignored in drugs fight', Times Education Supplement, 30 May 1997.

[49] Anderson, M, 1995, *Today's families in historical context*, quoted in Utting D, 1995, *Family and parenthood*, Joseph Rowntree Foundation, York, 42.